AFRICAN
CRAFTS

AFRICAN CRAFTS

Fun Things to Make and Do from West Africa

LYNNE GARNER

Chicago Review Press

**This book is dedicated to Aklowa
(The Traditional African Cultural Village)**

I would like to thank the following people, without whose help this book would not have been possible: Felix and Helen Cobbson for their insight and Felix's proofreading skills; Honorary Nana Len (Hobson), Honorary Queen Mum Rachel (Hobson), and Chris Bullen for being great travel companions; Robert B. Owusa (for his time and patience during my stay in Ghana); Jon my fiancé for his continued support and understanding; Matthew E. F. Rodriguez-Payne for his supply of very useful "useless" information; the staff of Saffron Walden museum for their time and for allowing me to photograph some of their African collection; the kente weavers of Bonwire; the adinkra printers of Ntonso; and the ladies of the Onyardze Pot Makers Co-op Assoc. for a wonderful day.

Library of Congress Cataloging-in-Publication Data
Is available from the Library of Congress.

First published in 2004 by The British Museum Press
A division of The British Museum Company Ltd
38 Russell Square, London WC1B 3QQ

Editor: Diana Briscoe
Designed and typeset by Terry Woodley
Printed and bound in China by C&C Offset.

Published in the United States by
Chicago Review Press, Incorporated
814 North Franklin Street
Chicago, Illinois 60610
ISBN-13: 978-1-55652-748-7
ISBN-10: 1-55652-748-9

5 4 3 2 1

CONTENTS

HOW IT ALL BEGAN

I first became interested in African crafts when I visited Aklowa at Takeley in eastern England. My main job involves working with all kinds of crafts, so I am always looking for new things to do and try.

Aklowa is a complete copy of a Ghanaian village, where you can see different West African buildings. There is also a large pond complete with dug-out canoe. It was started in 1977 by a Ghanaian teacher named Felix Cobbson. He wanted to let English people experience the African way of life. If you go there, you can take part in dancing, drumming sessions, crafts, and African cooking. I enjoyed myself so much that I returned several times and then spent some time developing activities for the children who came on school trips.

Eventually I got so interested that I decided to go to Ghana on a "fact finding" trip with a group of

Mask made by Bamum people of Cameroon. Masks like this are worn on top of the head and are thought to represent the king. The swollen face shows how well fed the king is.

I met this girl, who was looking after her baby brother, when we visited a market in Accra.

These children came to greet us when we visited Onyardze. I was overwhelmed by how pleased everyone was to meet us.

This bonfire has been lit to fire some pots. See chapter 2 for the full story.

I saw this little girl, who was selling bread, in a street market in Accra, the capital of Ghana.

other interested people. I wanted to see for myself how these arts and crafts fitted into their original cultures. It was the adventure of a lifetime, particularly visiting the various villages that specialized in potting, weaving, or block-printing.

Some of the crafts in this book relate to everyday life, such as pots for eating and drinking, or cloth to wear. Others, such as the masks, are used only at special ceremonies, lending them awe and mystery. However, the mask is only one part of such an event. The dancing and the music are just as important. All the elements are needed to make a complete picture. I have found that looking at something in a museum gives you only a part of what these objects mean to their makers and users.

Much of what you will encounter in the way of African art and crafts is made for sale to visitors. It is not for local people to use. However, these mass-produced pieces have been inspired by the beliefs and lifestyle of African people. I hope that this book will give you a small insight into the skill of the craftsmen and women that I met in Ghana.

Lynne Garner

Musician playing a gome drum with his hands and feet.

Boys make their own music with the aid of bottle tops tied to their boots.

WEST AFRICA AND GHANA: A BRIEF HISTORY

West Africa can be divided into three geographical zones running across from east to west. At the top in the north is the Sahara desert. In the middle is the Sahel, which is semi-desert turning into savanna (grassland with trees). In the south is woodland and forest.

European states imposed today's national borders when they colonized the area in the nineteenth century. Before that, many parts of West Africa had their own kingdoms and empires.

Modern Ghana is named after the ancient empire of Ghana that flourished between the fifth and eleventh centuries. However, ancient Ghana lay far to the north, in present-day Mauritania. The first Europeans arrived in modern Ghana in 1482 when Portuguese traders built a fort on the coast at Elmina. They started by trading for ivory and gold. Previously, these goods had reached Europe by being carried across the Sahara.

When the Europeans began to settle the Americas, they needed people to cultivate it for them. So they began to buy men and women from Africa to use as slaves. British, Dutch, Danish, and Portuguese slave traders took about 10,000 slaves a year from Africa to the Americas for over 250 years. They paid for the slaves with cloth and guns, which the Asante people of southern Ghana (among others) needed to build their empire, rich in gold and slaves.

This market stall in Accra had various types of musical instruments for sale.

A double-spouted pot made by the Bron people of Ghana.

Britain was the first country to abolish its slave trade in 1807, but it was only in 1870 that the last slave ship left West Africa. That was five years after the United States freed its slaves. The kingdom of the Asante was finally conquered by the British in 1900, after long and fierce resistance.

Under the British, the area was known as the Gold Coast. In the early twentieth century, it was very prosperous because it became a major source of cocoa, the main ingredient of chocolate. Ghana changed its name in 1957 when it became independent. It was the first country in Africa south of the Sahara to gain its independence. Ghana is still the world's second largest producer of cocoa, after Côte d'Ivoire (Ivory Coast), its neighbor to the west.

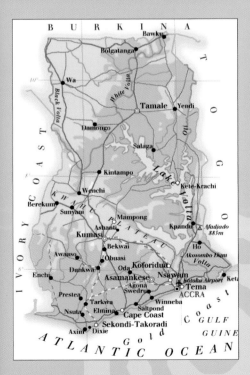

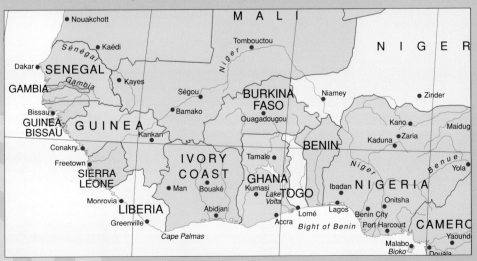

ADINKRA BLOCK PRINTING

Adinkra block printing.

In West African crafts, one village will often specialize in one craft. So when someone needs a new adinkra block-printed cloth, they know exactly where to go. Adinkra printing is generally done by men. Boys learn their skills from another male member of their family. A master printer must also be able to carve his blocks (stamps) and make his own dye.

Our guide had organized a trip to Ntonso, a village renowned for its adinkra block-printed cloths. After a long and exciting drive, watching admiringly as the driver blew his horn yet again to warn the vehicle in front we were about to pass, we finally arrived. I felt just like a child with a new toy, as I watched the printers practicing this craft under a large canvas awning beside the road.

Adinkra clothes drying by the roadside in Ntonso.

Stamp blocks are carved from a gourd.

HOW AN ADINKRA CLOTH IS CREATED

An adinkra cloth starts life as a large piece of pre-dyed cotton fabric. The printer lays it out on a piece of flat clean ground, and weighs or pegs it down. The fabric is then decorated using a comb and hand-carved blocks to print the stamped designs. The dye is made by boiling a mixture of tree bark and lumps of iron slag for several hours.

Once the cloth has been pegged out, the printer marks it out into squares. He uses a comb to draw a grid directly on to the cloth. The designs are then stamped in each of the grid squares. Finally the cloth is left to dry, hanging on a simple wooden frame in the sun. This wooden frame also serves as a "shop window" for people passing by.

The stamp blocks used to print the designs are made from pieces of calabash or gourd. First the gourd is cut in half and the inner flesh is removed. Then a design is carved into the hard outer skin. Three sticks are pushed into the back of the stamp block before it is left to dry. The sticks are then bound together at the other end to make a handle.

Adinkra designs can be found everywhere in Ghana: on modern clothes, plates, bowl and mugs, and even painted on walls. By the end of my research trip, I am sure the rest of my party were fed up each time I pointed out one of these designs, showing off even more when I could remember what its name or meaning was (see
page 15 for some examples).

Printing adinkra cloth beside the road. Note the lines of combing that make up the grid.

Skilled printers roll their stamp blocks to print the design.

PRINT YOUR OWN ADINKRA CLOTH

Before you can print your own adinkra cloth, you have to make the stamps to print it with. The easiest way to make a stamp is to cut it from a potato. You can also use foam ceiling tiles or the base of a Styrofoam container, or you could use the stamps from a children's stamping kit.

1 If you find the potato too tough, ask a grown-up to cut it in half for you.

2 Blot the juice from the flat cut side of the potato with the tissue.

3 Draw your design with the felt-tip pen on the flat surface.

3 Draw the design on the flat surface of a potato block.

4 Cut the design out of the potato block.

4 Cut away the potato from the outside of the design with the table knife. You now have a raised section that you can use to print with.

Be careful not to cut into the edge of your design. If you do, it will weaken your potato block and the design will begin to break up during use.

TO MAKE A POTATO STAMP:
You will need:
- Large raw potato
- Tissue
- Felt tip pen AND
- Table knife OR
- Cookie cutter

ANOTHER WAY TO CUT THE STAMP:

1 Place the cookie cutter upside down on the flat surface. Put the cut side of the half potato on top. Push it down about a half inch (1 cm). If you go all the way in, don't worry.

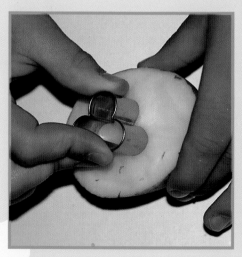

1 Press a cookie cutter into the surface of the potato.

2 *Cut away the potato from the outside of the cookie cutter.*

2 Carefully cut away the potato around the outside of the cutter with the table knife.

3 Remove the cutter. You will then have a raised section to print with.

TIP If you cannot finish your block printing at one time, you can save your stamp to use another day.

Put it in a sealed plastic bag, or wrap it well in plastic wrap, and put it in the fridge. You can use your potato stamp for several days if you store it like this.

USING YOUR STAMP:

You will need:

- Newspaper to cover work surface
- Cotton cloth (washed and ironed)
- 4 weights
- Carved potato stamp
- T-shirt painting dye or dye inkpad
- Sponge and soup plate (if using T-shirt dye)
- Large toothed comb

1 Find a large flat surface to do your stamping on. Check with a grown-up before you start to make sure that it is OK to use it.

2 Cover your work surface with newspaper.

3 Lay out your cloth and weigh down the corners with the four weights.

USING T-SHIRT DYE:

4 Pour a little of your dye into the soup plate. Put the top back on and put the bottle where you cannot knock it over by accident.

5 *Dip the teeth of the comb into the dye. Tap off any excess dye.*

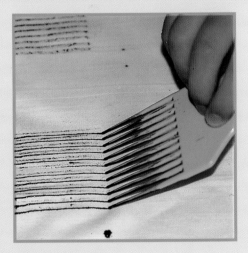

5 *Drawing one row of the grid.*

5 Dip the comb's teeth into the dye, then tap off any excess. Now draw a series of straight lines across your cloth.

6 Repeat this, leaving about a 2-inch (5 cm) gap between each set of lines, until you get to the bottom of the cloth.

7 Now draw more sets of lines from top to bottom about 2 inches (5 cm) apart, until you have drawn a grid. Make sure the squares are large enough to take one or more prints from your stamp.

7 About three-quarters of the way through drawing the grid.

8 Dab the sponge into your dye. Gently tap the sponge on the surface of your stamp. Check there is a good even coverage of ink before you start stamping. If there is too much dye, very gently scrape a little off on the edge of the soup plate.

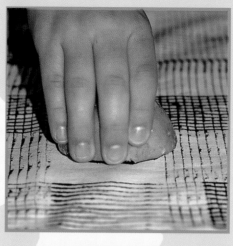

9 Stamp in the center of the square.

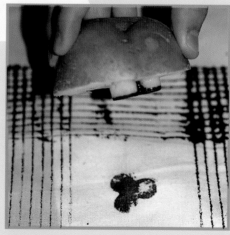

9 Lift it off straight upward.

9 Carefully put your stamp into the center of one of the blank squares of your cloth. Press it down firmly. Count to three and lift it off straight upward. Try not to rock the stamp or it may smudge.

10 Repeat until all the squares are stamped. You will have to reapply dye to your stamp every two or three times you use it.

11 Leave the cloth to dry. Look on page 16 to find out how to wear it properly.

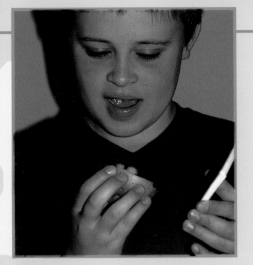

2 *Blow gently across the inked stamp before using it.*

IF YOU USE A DYE INKPAD:

1 Hold the stamp in one hand and the inkpad in the other. Gently tap the surface of the stamp against the pad. If the pad is smaller than the stamp, then move the inkpad around the stamp surface until it is all inked.

2 Hold the stamp up to the light and check that the surface has a good even coverage of ink.

3 Blow very gently across the inked surface before putting it on to the cloth. This ensures that the ink is ready to be printed.

Then follow steps 9 to 11 opposite.

Adinkra cloths are stamped with traditional designs. There are 53 recognized designs, and each has its own name and meaning. If you look closely at the stamps' surfaces, you will see each one is a slightly different color. This is because they are carved by hand from gourds. Here are some popular designs:

Awia ne Bosome means "Sun and Moon"

Afafanto Ntaban means "Wings of the Butterfly"

Abeti Ntoma means "Shoulder's Cloth" (or piled on a shoulder—how it is worn by men)

Atamfo Atwameho means "Enemies Surround Me"

Akonfuna means "Cross Swords" (chiefs)

Nsoroma means "Star"

Gyenyame means "God, the Omnipotent"

Akoma means "Heart"

Owuo Atwedie means "Death's Ladder"

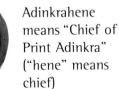

Adinkrahene means "Chief of Print Adinkra" ("hene" means chief)

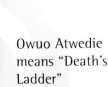

HOW TO WEAR AN ADINKRA CLOTH

1 Hang one long side of the cloth over your shoulders. Grasp the top edge with each hand as far along as you can reach and center yourself in it.

2 Let your left arm drop a little and twist so that the cloth covers it. Take the other side under your right armpit. Keep the cloth tight all the time.

3 Drape the cloth in your right hand over your left arm, so that your front is covered. You need about a 1-foot (30 cm) overlap.

4 Pleat the front side of the cloth up onto your shoulder, so that it hangs down your back. Do the same with the back, so that it hangs down your front. Fold in the edges under your arm tidily.

CLOTHES FOR SPECIAL OCCASIONS

We all have our own styles of clothes for special occasions. Adinkra cloths are worn on special occasions in southern Ghana. The cloths are covered in designs which have meanings based upon proverbs or show everyday objects.

The background color decides the type of occasion where the cloth is worn. Dark colors, such as black or brown, are worn at sad occasions like funerals. Red is worn by people in mourning. The word "adinkra" actually means "farewell." Other background colors include green, purple, blue, and white. Lighter colors are worn on joyful occasions, such as a baby's naming ceremony or a wedding.

Unlike kente cloth (see pages 38–45),

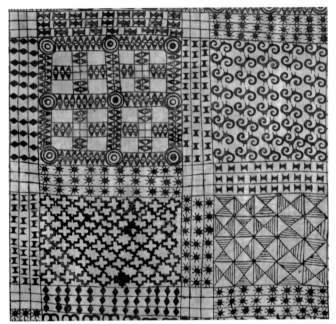

A section of the adinkra cloth collected by T. E. Bowditch in 1817.

A collection of adinkra stamps from the British Museum displays a few of the hundreds of different designs.

adinkra cloth is quick to produce, so many more people can afford to buy it. It is one reason why it is worn by many people in Ghana today. One of the oldest surviving adinkra cloths is in the British Museum. A traveler named T. E. Bowditch collected it in 1817.

Many of the ancient adinkra designs have gained new meanings in modern times. For example, the ram's horn design, which originally meant "victory in war," is taken by Christians today to mean the victory of life over death.

POT COILING

I was very keen to discover how pots were made in Ghana. A two-hour car drive from Accra took us to a community that was very different from the hustle and bustle of the capital city.

At last, we stopped at a small cluster of houses. We waited in the shade of some trees while smiling children peeked at us from behind tree trunks. When we looked up the dusty track, we saw the whole village of Onyardze coming to greet us. People with painted bodies and strange hats emerged from the heat haze dancing, drumming, and singing as a special welcome to us. We walked up to the meeting house with them where the village elders and their interpreters greeted us. Then we were taken to see some of the village women who were busy making pots. The people of West Africa use pots for storing food or water, cooking, and preparing food. They are all completely made by hand. Pot making is women's work. Every woman in a village will make pots—the skills are passed on from mother to daughter. Normally women make pots in their own homes, but they were delighted to show off their craft and their years of experience.

This finely decorated pot was made by the Lobi people of Burkina Fasso.

Building the bottom of a large pot.

Shaping the rim of a large pot.

HOW POTS ARE MADE IN GHANA

I had been taught how to make pots by coiling in England. My teacher told me to work from the base upward. However, in Ghana, they generally build the top first and add the base later. When the pot is finished, they beat it with a spatula to produce a smooth shape.

Next they burnish (polish) the outside with a smooth stone or a similar object so the pot is "sealed." Burnishing improves the look of the finished pot, and also makes the pot hold liquids better—Ghanaian potters do not use glaze on their pots. Any decoration can be added at this point—lines, dots, and other simple symbols cut into the clay are popular. I was fascinated to see an eaten corn cob used as a burnisher.

Once the pot has dried out in the hot sun, it is fired in a bonfire, a process that again takes much skill. The women

Closing off the hole in the base of a large pot.

The sun-dried pots are stacked together and a bonfire is built over the top.

Smoothing the surface of the pot.

19

This woman is stoking the bonfire with the help of a long stick.

Once the bonfire is out and the pots have cooled, they are ready for use. Some pots break during firing, so you very rarely end up with the number you started with.

started by piling sticks into a cone. Then they placed the first batch of pots around it. They built up layers of pots and dry grasses, branches, and leaves until the bonfire was complete. The bonfire was controlled by sprinkling water on it to regulate the heat and create an even burn. Up to 120 pots are fired at a time to save time, effort, and wood.

The best time to light the fire is about three to four P.M. At that time, a cool breeze picks up as the sun comes lower in the sky. If it is too windy, the bonfire will not burn evenly. If there is no wind, then the bonfire may not get hot enough.

However, the bonfire was lit around midday for our visit. The temperature was well over 86°F (30°C), so standing close to it became very difficult. The women tending the fire were amused when I stepped back and shaded my face from the heat. I was very glad my camera had a zoom lens.

Another finely decorated pot made in Cameroon (see the map on page 9).

COIL YOUR OWN POTS

1 Turn the tray upside down and cover its base with paper. You will use it as the base to build your pot on.

2 Open the packet of air-dry clay and cut about 2 inches (5 cm) off one end. Put the remaining clay in the plastic bag or box and seal it carefully.

You will need:
- Small tray
- Paper to cover tray
- Air-drying clay
- Table knife
- Self-sealing plastic bag or airtight plastic box
- Flat stick or spatula
- Large smooth stone or a metal spoon
- Newspaper
- Acrylic paints
- Paint brush

3 Roll the clay between your hands until it becomes soft and pliable. Then roll it into a large, thick sausage.

5 *Start squeezing and pulling a section of the clay upward.*

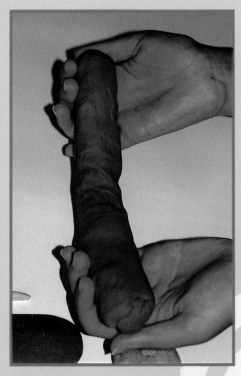

3 *Roll the clay between your hands to make a large, thick sausage.*

4 *Smooth the two ends together carefully, so you can't see where it joins together.*

4 Coil this sausage of clay into a circle and squeeze the two ends together. Smooth the join carefully until you can hardly see where it was.

5 Squeeze one section of the clay between your fingers and thumb, pulling it upward as you do so. Remember to support the clay inside and outside as you work around.

If it does collapse, it is probably easiest to roll the clay into a ball and start again.

6 Keep working around the edge to make it taller and thinner.

6 Keep pulling and squeezing the clay upward, until it is about ½ inch (1 cm) thick and about 2 to 2 ½ inches (5–6 cm) high.

7 Round off the top edge with your flat stick to shape the rim of the pot. You can use your fingers if you find that easier.

8 Smooth the surface of the pot with the damp sponge. Do it very carefully both inside and out—if you press too hard, it will collapse. If it does, press it very gently back into shape.

9 Put the tray in a cool, dry place and leave the rim section to dry out for one to two hours. Keep checking because the bottom edge must not get too dry.

10 As soon as the rim is dry enough to take the weight of the bottom section, turn it over so that it is sitting rim-edge down. Stuff it with newspaper for extra support.

11 Cut the same amount of clay from the block and repeat steps 2 and 3. Put the rest of the clay back in its plastic bag or box.

12 Repeat steps 4, 5, and 6, until the clay is about ½ inch (1 cm) thick and about 2 to 2 ½ inches (5–6 cm) high.

13 Gently and carefully start to work the clay in toward the center until the hole is about a ½ inch (1.5 cm) across.

13 Work the clay in toward the center to make the base.

14 Try to squeeze and pull the clay to close the hole. If you can't close it completely, cut and roll another small piece of clay into a flat disc

10 Stuff the top of the pot for extra support before starting to make the bottom section.

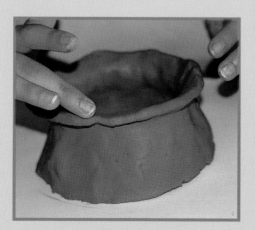

7 Flatten the rim outwards.

to form the base of your pot. Lay it over the hole and press the edges gently together to seal the bottom.

If you press too hard, it will collapse, but you can press it very gently back into shape.

15 Place the damp base on top of the dry rim section. Gently mold the base to fit the firmer top section. Leave it to dry for one hour.

16 Remove the newspaper. Very carefully smooth out the joins both inside and out. Be careful: if you press too hard, it will collapse.

17 You can use different shaped objects to stamp decorations into the damp clay (see page 24 for some ideas).

18 Leave the pot to dry fully in a cool place—this will take several days.

19 If you haven't stamped patterns into the clay, you can paint the dried pot with color bands. Or look at the pots in this chapter for some other ideas.

14 *Press the clay disc into position very gently.*

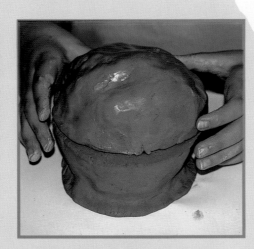

15 *Mold the damp base section to match the top section.*

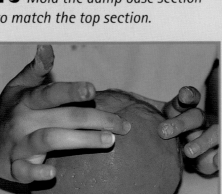

14 *Smooth the join line of the clay disc to seal the base.*

16 *Smooth the joins, particularly in the middle.*

18 *Impress decorative shapes into the clay (see page 24).*

STAMPING PATTERNS

You can use all sorts of objects as stamps for your pot. Here are some ideas to start you off, but look around your home and see what you can find.

Always ask for permission before using something that doesn't belong to you.

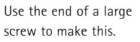

The point of a pencil will make a small circle

The other end will make a larger one.

Use the end of a large screw to make this.

Use the end of a tube to make something like this.

You can also experiment with bits of jewelry, a piece of Lego, a very small doll—try making a hand or footprint—and almost anything else you can think of.

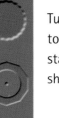

The end of a nail file will make a small triangle.

Use the end of a bolt to make a square.

Use the end of a highlighter for this oval shape.

Use a square stamp turned on its side to make a diamond.

Tube caps and bottle tops often make good stamps with unusual shapes.

If you get a chance to make pots that can be fired, do try it out. You can make a pot just as we have described and then get it fired in a kiln.

BYGONE TRADITIONS

Not all African pots were made for cooking or storage. Some were made for use in religious ceremonies. Others were made as part of the goods that a bride would bring to her marriage—of course, they would be used after the wedding.

They were not all plain shapes either. In various parts of Africa, pots are made with the body of a man or woman forming the top of a jug. They also used clay to sculpt complicated figures, though these were usually made by men.

The Asante people of southern Ghana used to make "family pots." These were used as part of the funeral ceremonies of important people. The pots were black and had a lid. They were decorated with a variety of images including birds, human heads, and spiders (Anansi, the clever tricky spider, is an important character in

This bottle for water or beer was made by the Igbo people of Nigeria.

Ghanaian folktales).

The ceremony required members of a family to shave their heads and put their hair into this pot. Then, at sunset, some women of the family took this pot to the "place of the pots" where it was left, along with a food offering. Unlike cooking pots, these "family pots" were made by men or by women who were too old to have children.

A Better Taste!
A teacher friend of mine, who had many students from Africa, told me that they often brought ceramic cooking pots with them from home. They said that metal saucepans made the food taste of metal —even the non-stick ones.

The water pot at the back is a traditional shape and was made by the Gwari people in Nigeria. The front pot is also used for water. It is decorated with Gwari animal designs, but was made at a craft center in Abuja in central Nigeria.

MASK MAKING

I first came across African masks during a visit to the market near our hotel. Having only gone to see what was being sold—I intended to come back nearer the end of my visit—I didn't have any money with me. However, the stall holders were quite happy to trade with me for my Mickey Mouse watch, and in the end I was able to buy two masks and a carved statuette. All the masks and other traditional wares were made and sold by local craftsmen.

My second experience of a mask came during my visit to Onyardze (see pages 8–9). Our group was greeted by music and dance. One of the villagers decided to wear a "mask" in our honor. As he did not have a traditional mask with him that was suitable, he created one on the spot. He used an orange builder's helmet and a large false mustache, showing us visitors both the importance of mask wearing and the cunning of the wearer.

Masks hanging on a market stall ready for sale to tourists.

Gold mask made by the Asante people of southern Ghana.

MASKS OF AFRICA

I was absolutely fascinated by the many designs of masks that had come from all over Africa. I discovered that there are rock paintings in the Sahara desert made by the Tassili people that seem to show people wearing masks. These may be 8,000 years old. From the other end of the continent, there are rock paintings by the San people in the

A masker from Nigeria, photographed in the 1940s.

Drackensburg Mountains of South Africa. These show masked hunters.

West Africa has thousands of shapes and styles of masks. They can be made of wood, metal, leather, cloth, or leaves and grasses. Some just cover the face—others are like helmets. Others still are tied on top of the head. They range in size from the tiny masks of the Dan people of Côte d'Ivoire to the giant masks of the Baga people of Guinea. These last are so heavy, they have to be carried on the masker's shoulders.

Masks are used for many purposes in West Africa, but often they form part of a ritual dance or parade. The masker can also have an elaborate costume, which covers his whole body. Generally men were the only people who were allowed to wear or even see masks. In some societies women were killed if they saw a mask. However, the women of the Mende people in Sierra Leone and Liberia wear masks as part of their secret societies' rituals.

Masks are treated with respect when not being worn for a ceremony. In Nigeria, they are hung up in a special room only used for rituals and the storing of masks.

A wooden helmet mask made by the Mende people of Sierra Leone. This is the only mask in this book to be owned and used solely by women.

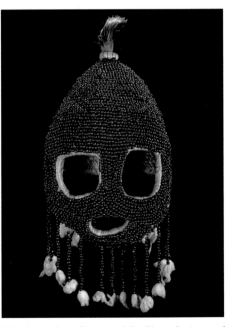

Mask made of vegetable fiber, hair, and poisonous red abrus seeds. Probably used by the Angas people of northern Nigeria in one of their dance societies.

This mask was made by the Bamana people of Mali (see page 9). The Bamanas' tribal lore is passed on by various men's societies, known as jow. This female mask belongs to the N'tomo jow.

MAKING YOUR OWN MASK

1 You can make a mask to be painted or give it a lion's mane. Blow up the balloon to the size required. Tie a piece of string around the knot of the balloon.

2 Mix equal quantities of the glue and warm water in a large bowl. (For example, if you have 8 oz of glue, you will need 8 oz of water to mix with it.)

3 Tear the newspaper into small pieces—about 1 inch (3 cm) square is best. Don't cut the paper because the torn edges knit together better.

4 *Starting to cover the balloon—about 1/4 of the way through.*

4 Soak the newspaper pieces in the glue for about 3 minutes. Then begin to cover the surface of the balloon. Don't cover the whole balloon, just until you have something a little larger than the size and shape of the finished mask.

5 Leave it to dry for 10 minutes, then put on a second and third layer of newspaper. Let the mask dry for 10 minutes each time.

6 Dip whole sheets of tissue paper into the glue and water mixture and remove at once.

> **TO MAKE YOUR OWN MASK:**
> You will need:
> • Pear-shaped balloon
> • String
> • Water-soluble glue
> • Large bowl
> • Warm water
> • Newspaper
> • Tissue paper
> • Brown paper
> • Scissors
> • Paint
> • Clear varnish
> • Artist's brush
> • Hole punch
> • Raffia (optional)

3 *Tear the newspaper into rough squares.*

6 *Mold the eyebrows and nose, and put them in position.*

Scrunch them into a block and start molding the face. You may find it easier to do the nose first, then you can be sure you have left enough space for the eyes above and the mouth below.

7 When the face looks the way you want it, put on another two layers of newspaper pieces as in steps 3–5.

7 *Add two more layers of newspaper over the eyebrows and nose.*

8 Now tear the brown paper —you can reuse old brown envelopes—into small pieces and soak them as before (they may need a little longer in the glue). Then cover the whole mask with a layer of brown paper.

9 Use the string to tether the balloon somewhere that is safe while it dries out completely. This will take at least 24 hours.

10 When the mask is dry, let down the balloon. Ask an adult to cut out the mouth and the eyeholes, using a craft knife or a pair of very sharp scissors. Then trim the edge of the mask so that it fits your face.

10 *Trim the edge of the mask with scissors.*

11 Paint the mask to match one shown here or make up your own design. Let the paint dry completely.
If the mask is for display, you can varnish it (see step 12).

11 *You can paint the mask with any design you like.*

11/12 *Carefully varnish the mask if you want to display it.*

12 Or you can just paint a coat of clear varnish over the brown paper. Make sure the varnish is really dry before you do anything else to the mask.

MASK MAKING

15 *Use one side of the hole punch to make holes for the lion's mane.*

16 *Tie lengths of raffia all around to make the lion's mane.*

13 Punch one hole on either side of your mask just above where your ears are.

14 Cut two lengths of raffia about 2 feet (60 cm) long. Double one length in two, then thread it through the hole on one side. Bring the ends back through the loop and gently pull it tight. Repeat on the opposite side. Now you can tie the mask on or hang it up.

15 If you would like to give your mask a lion's mane, use one side of the hole punch to make holes all around the outer edge. They should be about ¼ inch (5 mm) away from

the edge and about ¾ inch (2 cm) apart.

16 Cut the rest of the raffia into 1 foot (30 cm) lengths. Tie them on all the way around.

WEST AFRICAN MASKS

Seven maskers of noble birth, who also carry ceremonial swords, wear these brass helmet masks. They dance back and forth before the Oba of Benin, Nigeria, seven times as a sign of their loyalty.

Only a few old masks survive because the materials used to make them were often fragile. Many were intended to last only for a short time. They were destroyed when no longer needed. Most surviving ancient masks are made of wood or metal.

The design of a mask is traditional. The masker had to follow these traditions and also work in great secrecy. Masks always have a supernatural origin, so the masker will say "It was found in the bush" or "It was given by a spirit, a long time ago."

In the Côte d'Ivoire (see map on page 9), if a mask was damaged or destroyed, a small copy was made as a temporary home for the spirit of the mask. The spirit would then show itself in a dream to the masker who then had to find a sculptor to carve a new mask.

Sometimes masks represent the spirits of the ancestors. At other times, they represent monsters who wish to attack the human world. Some of the most scary are the spirits of the initiation ritual. They lurk along the way as a boy goes through the secret ceremonies that turn him into a man.

Not all masks have a serious use. In some ceremonies, a masked clown will act as the emcee, introducing each mask as it appears. In between, the masker makes rude jokes about local chiefs and other officials and about recent scandals.

Carved wooden mask by the Yoruba people from Nigeria. It shows a warrior on horseback.

This ivory mask was worn by the Oba (king) of Benin in Nigeria, probably around his neck. It is nine and a half inches (24.5 cm) high. The top is decorated with heads of Portuguese people, recognizing Benin's treaties with them. This mask dates from the sixteenth century.

MUSIC MAKERS

Music making in all its forms is very important to the people of Ghana. During my visit there, our group was treated to many forms of entertainment. Ghanaians are rightly proud of their musical heritage and take every opportunity to show it off. Music surrounded us at almost every meal, and musical instruments were on sale in most of the markets we visited. We often saw musicians trying these instruments out. All the instruments on sale were made using local materials.

African music emphasizes rhythm. Interlocking rhythms are created within a piece of music using various types of drums and other percussion instruments, such as shakers and bells. However, we saw lots of other musical instruments, including ones similar to guitars and harps.

This is a donno or 'talking' drum from Nigeria. They are used for sending messages.

Drums at a market ready for sale.

This drummer led the dancing by the people of Onyardze (see page 8).

MUSIC IN WEST AFRICA

Xylophones and similar types of music makers are common in West Africa, where hardwoods are available to make the bars. The bars are strung on a wooden frame with small gourds fastened underneath. These act as resonators (sound magnifiers) for the bars. They are played with a padded stick.

The shaker, called an axatse (say a-ha-chay), is made from a hollowed out gourd covered in a net strung with beads or seeds. You hold it in one hand and beat it against the palm of the other hand.

The gonje is also made from a gourd, which is cut in half and hollowed out Then it has a skin stretched across the open front and a neck added with one string. You pluck the string with one hand while the other hand controls the pitch by pressing down on the string along the neck.

Musician playing an axatse.

A gyil (a type of xylophone) from northern Ghana.

There are many types of drums and each one has a special use. The gankogui drum is used to set a regular beat and to keep the musicians together. This instrument is held in one hand and struck with a stick. It gives two different sounds, depending on where you hit it.

Drummers in action.

The donno drum (sometimes called the "talking" drum) is widely used in Ghana, especially by the Asante people. These drums can be used to send messages. They are carved from a single piece of wood with goat-hide "skin" (the drum's head or playing surface) tied on with leather thongs. When the thongs are squeezed under the player's arm, it tightens the skin and that changes the note of the drum. It is played with a curved stick.

33

MAKE YOUR OWN DRUM

TO MAKE YOUR OWN DRUM:
You will need:

- Large tin can about 8 inches (20 cm) across (a large coffee tin works well)
- Can opener
- Plastic or sticky fabric tape (Scotch tape)
- Plain white paper
- Paint and brushes or colored pencils
- Double-sided sticky tape
- Hole punch
- Heavy duty plastic (pond liner or thick garbage bag)
- Rubber band
- Strong thin string about 15 yards (12 m) long
- Scissors
- Blunt needle with big eye

1 Wash the tin can carefully and dry it thoroughly. Ask a grown-up to cut the bottom off, using the can opener.

2 Use the tape to cover the sharp cut edge of the tin can. Be very careful while doing this so you don't cut yourself.

3 Cut a piece of paper that will wrap right around the drum. Color it or paint it. Then use the double-sided tape to stick it onto the tin.

2 Use the plastic tape to cover the sharp edge at the bottom of the can.

3 Paint or color the paper to decorate your drum.

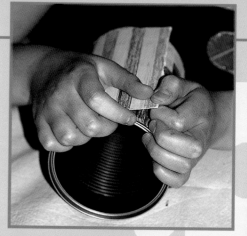

3 Use double-sided tape to fix one end of the paper to the can, then tape the other end for a tight fit.

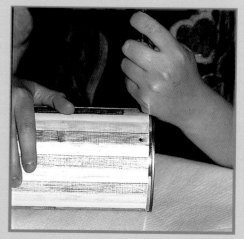

4 Use one side of the hole punch to make holes in the tin can.

4 Use the hole punch to make a series of holes around the tin just above your tape edging about ½ inch (1.5 cm) apart.

5 Cut a circle from the plastic, 2 inches (5 cm) bigger than the drum's top, to make the skin.

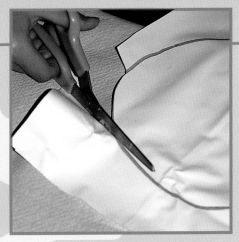

5 *Cutting out the plastic skin—use the can as a guide to the size.*

6 Cut a length of string that will go twice around the can and have 4 inches (10 cm) left over.

7 Place the skin over the end of the drum, opposite to the end with the holes. Use the rubber band to hold it steady.

8 Tie the string around the drum over the plastic to hold it in place. The string sits about 1 inch (2.5 cm) below the top edge. Don't knot it too tight as you must thread the needle under it. Take off the rubber band.

9 Tie a large knot at one end of the rest of the string. Thread the other end through one hole at the base of the drum so the knot is inside. Now thread it into the needle.

10 Fold the bottom edge of the plastic back on itself. Use the end of the needle to pierce a hole through both pieces above the string line.

8 *Thread the ends of the string under the knot to make it neat.*

11 Push the needle and long string under the doubled plastic and its string band, and bring it out through the two holes you have just made.

7 *Use the rubber band to position the skin on the drum at first.*

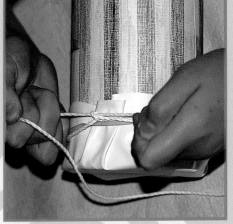

9 *Tying the skin on to the drum. The rubber band holds it in place.*

12 *Threading the long string through a bottom hole.*

12 Take the long string down to the next-door hole to the one with the knot, thread it in through that, and out of the next one along.

13 Take the string up to the skin and repeat steps 11 and 12. Continue until you reach the hole with the knot.

14 Now you can tune your drum by tightening or loosening the string. When you are happy with the sound, tie off the string tightly inside the drum.

15 Trim the string ends and the plastic, if needed, to make the drum look neat and tidy.

14 Tuning the drum by tightening or loosening the string.

PLAYING YOUR DRUM:

The way you hit the drum skin allows you to make various sounds.

- OPEN SOUND: hit the edge of the drum with a flat hand.
- CUPPED SOUND: hit the drum with a cupped hand.
- CLOSED SOUND: is produced in two ways. Hit the drum skin with the flat of your hand and leave your hand on the skin. Or you can lay one hand on the drum skin while hitting it with your other hand.

   With a drum stick, you can hit the skin with the stick and leave the stick pressed firmly on the skin (rather than bouncing off again).

MUSIC IN GHANA TODAY

There are two kinds of music played in Ghana today. The first is traditional, the second is social music. It is played at social gatherings (just as we play pop at a party). Traditional music is often played at a ceremony—to celebrate a good harvest or remember someone who has died. Each tune is tied to that ceremony. Players cannot alter the music or how it is played, which is handed down to them.

The *Hatsiatsia* is a traditional ceremony performed by the Ewé (say *you-eh*) people. This dance is believed to wash away disagreements and arguments, and to bring greater unity to the villagers, who live and work close together. Everyone in the village takes part. The music is played on two different types of metal bell. First a bucket of water is blessed and placed within the circle of dancers. A shuffling step takes each dancer around the bucket. As they pass it, they dip their hands into the water and wipe their faces. Every so often, one dancer will take some water and spray it over as many people as he can.

Another Ewé ceremony is called the *Gota*. In it, couples compete to see who can dance the fastest and best. Sometimes the competition is between the musicians and the dancers. It needs three types of drums plus a bell and an axatse (shaker). The master drummer sets the speed of the music. As they dance, the dancers will sing words like, "Is this the best you can do?" This encourages the drummers to beat faster and faster. At last the dancers will admit defeat and change their song to, "OK, you win!"

This Asante-style drum was found in Virginia. It may have gone there on a slave ship.

A type of xylophone called a balafon from Burkina Fasso. The gourds under the bars make the sound louder.

This shaker was used in the manhood ceremonies of the Bamana people of Mali.

This wooden drum with iron rattles was made by the Dan people from Côte d'Ivoire and Liberia.

KENTE STRIP WEAVING

Kente is a kind of cloth made by the Asante and other peoples of central Ghana. It is woven in narrow strips up to five inches (13 cm) wide, on a strip loom. Each strip is

These Asante nobles are wearing kente cloths.

divided into blocks of different patterns in bright colors. The strips are then stitched together to make a large cloth with the patterns carefully lined up.

Kente cloth used to be worn only by rich and powerful people. Some designs belong exclusively to the king and chiefs of the Asante kingdom. Today it is worn as a symbol of national unity, and is still very expensive. When Ghana became independent in 1957, the first president, Kwama Nkrumah, started wearing kente cloth and other local clothes to show his commitment to the unity of the new country.

Bonwire, near the Asante capital of Kumasi, produces perhaps the best quality kente cloths. Local Members of Parliament have formed a co-operative in order to ensure the future of the kente cloth and those who spend their lives weaving it. These weavers are now encouraged to take up this ancient craft as a way of providing for themselves and their village. Looms are provided and the weavers work together in large sheds.

Visiting Bonwire was one of our biggest adventures. It took several hours of fast and furious driving.

Preparing the thread for weaving.

Close-up of a kente strip, showing two different effects.

At last, we turned off down a rough dirt track. As we bumped along, groups of people on foot waved a welcome.

In Bonwire, we were greeted by a group of inquisitive children who followed us to the large shed where the kente weavers work. One of the older weavers gave us a guided tour, patiently answering all my questions (which were translated by our guide).

Both men and women weave kente cloth today, although in the past only men were weavers. However, women often weave only for their own use. I asked one weaver why there were only men in the shed. He said that his wife could weave, but she spent her time caring for their family. He provided an income from his weaving skills.

In recent years, tourist interest has given the weavers

A kente strip with a modern pattern in progress.

new ways to earn a living. Today they make belts, bags, place mats and bedspreads from kente style strips. They do not use true kente designs—the weavers prefer to keep those for the more important cloths worn by local people.

Using a kente strip loom.

WEAVE A KENTE STRIP

TO MAKE A SIMPLE LOOM:
You will need:
- Medium weight cardboard
- Ruler
- Pencil
- Scissors

1 Mark out a rectangle measuring about 8 x 10 inches (20 x 25 cm) on a piece of cardboard. Cut out the shape.

2 *Cut V-shaped notches along the two short sides.*

2 Cut V-shapes along the short sides of the board, no more than 0.2 inches (5 mm) apart.

3 Cut a small slit in the first and last V-shape at one end (this is to anchor the wool thread in place).

TO WEAVE ON YOUR LOOM:
You will need:
- Wool, tapestry wool, or embroidery thread
- Large tapestry needle (or a wicking needle as used in candle making)
- Wide-toothed comb
- Scissors

1 Cut a long piece of wool at least 3 feet (1 m) long. Tie a knot at one end and pull it into the left-end slit.

2 Wind the wool around the back of the card and into the first notch at the far end. Bring it across the front to the second notch and then take it behind the card again. The wool should be tight but not stretched.

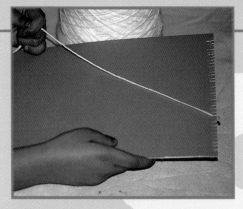

1 *Fix the knotted end of the wool into the slit in the end V-shape.*

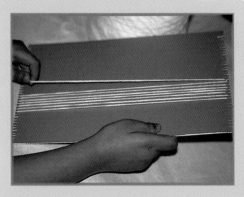

3 *Wind the wool round and round the card into the notches.*

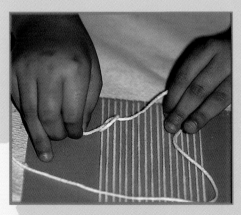

4 *Tie on more wool with a reef knot at the back.*

40

3 Continue wrapping the wool around the card until the strip is as wide as you need or until every notch is filled.

4 If you have to add another length of wool, tie the knot at the back of the card. Pull the wool into the slit in the last V-shape and knot it to finish.

5 Cut off about 2 feet (60 cm) of wool and thread the needle.

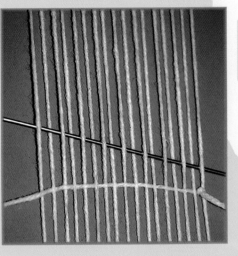

6 On the next row, weave under where you went over the first time.

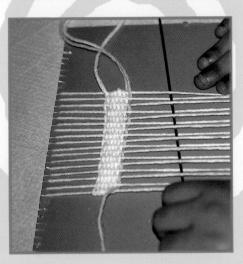

7 Use a comb to make sure the rows of wool lie tight together.

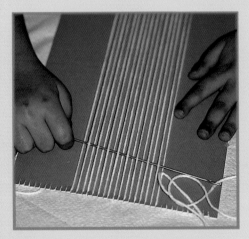

5 It is easier to do your weaving with a longer needle.

6 Weave the needle under the first strand of wool, then over the next. Continue weaving under, over, under, over, until you reach the last thread.

7 Weave the needle back to the side you started from. If the thread went under the last thread, then start over that thread as you weave back the other way.

8 Repeat steps 6 and 7 until you have completed your piece of weaving. **Do not pull the thread too tight.** If you do, then your strip will curve inward in the middle and the sides will not be straight.

9 As you weave, you can "beat in" the wool. Use the comb to push the wool up against the last row and make sure that it lies flat and straight.

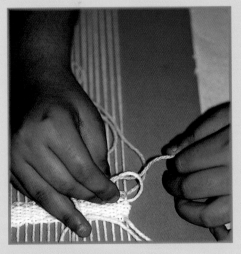

8 Always add a new strand of wool or a new color at an edge.

10 If you want to change color, or tie in a new strand of wool, always do it at an edge, not halfway across your strip.

■● *Use a reef knot to connect the two threads together.*

■■ *Thread some wool under the first and over the second thread.*

■■ *Take the wool back under the first thread to make a loop.*

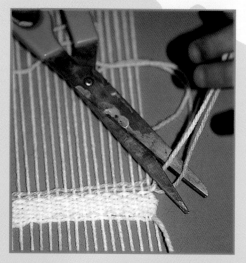

To finish off, thread a needle with a piece of wool. Weave the needle under the first thread, then back again (this will give you a loop). Now take the needle over the single thread and through the loop, then pull it tight.

12 Repeat until you reach the last thread, then tie a knot to finish off.

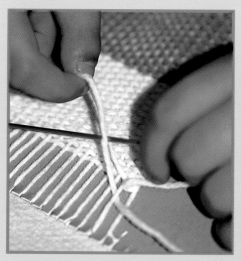

■● *Cut the ends off neatly with a pair of scissors.*

13 To remove your woven strip from the card, turn it over and cut the threads in the center of the back.

Wait until you have woven another three rows, then knot the two ends together with a reef knot, and trim them short.

14 Knot the long threads together in pairs to stop the weaving from coming apart.

■■ *Thread the wool through the loop and pull the knot tight.*

OTHER WEAVES

You have just learned how to do a plain weave. However, you can change the way your finished strip looks by changing the number of threads you travel over and under as you weave.

For example you could go over two threads and then under two, or another way is to go over two threads and under one thread.

You can also use different types of thread, such as silks or cottons, to alter the look of your weaving.

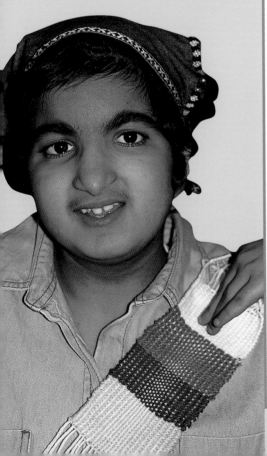

PATTERNS

Each pattern has a name. For example, kente cloths that contain many colors and vast numbers of different designs are called Adwinasa. This means "My skill is exhausted" or "My ideas have come to an end." Kente weavers use both new and old designs—new patterns are being invented all the time.

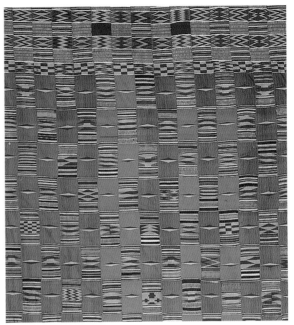

Section of a kente cloth.

Two famous old designs are called Atta Birago and Afua Kobi. These were named after two queen mothers of the Asante people. The designs were invented to honor them. Others are named after historical events or things you might find in your house.

Proverbs and sayings are an important part of African culture and this is reflected in some of the names given to kente designs. One design is called Nyawohoche (meaning "He has become rich"). This was supposed to be worn only by men who had more than $2,000 worth of gold dust.

Another design is known as the "liar's cloth" because it is woven in such a way that each side is different. It is said to have been designed to "confuse persons of doubtful veracity (truthfulness) who came before the the Asante king."

WEARING KENTE CLOTH

Men wear a kente cloth in two ways. The first is called Okatakyie, (meaning "brave man"), and this is used by chiefs. This way of wearing the kente cloth creates more volume during wear and gives a far more flamboyant look. The cloth is wound around the body and over the left shoulder. Any remaining length is rested upon the left arm.

The second way is called Kyere w'anantu (meaning "show your legs"). Men who wish to show off their physical development and grace use this style. The cloth is worn just above the knees, drawing more of the cloth up around the wearer's shoulders. Whichever style is used, it is always important that the patterned stripes are straight both horizontally and vertically and that the bottom edge is level and does not dip at any point.

A cloth takes an experienced weaver about three months to complete. The weaver must produce 18 strips measuring five inches (13 cm) wide and nine and a half feet (290 cm) long to weave a complete garment for a man. These strips are then sewn edge to edge in order to form a large kente cloth.

A woman will wear two cloths (one as a skirt and the other as a top). The two need 26 strips, averaging five inches (13 cm) wide and six feet (183 cm) long. Because it takes a lot of time to weave strips for a cloth, they are very expensive. Many people can only afford them by paying for a cloth by installments.

Two Asante nobles dressed in kente cloths.

This Ghanaian woman, dancing before her king, is wearing kente cloths.

THE HISTORY OF KENTE

The area of West Africa now known as Ghana is home to many peoples—two of whom are the Asante and the Ewé. Both of these peoples weave kente strip to make larger cloths.

There are two Asante stories that tell how kente weaving was brought to their lands. The first story tells how the first weaver, who was called Otah Kraban, brought back the loom to Bonwire from the Ivory Coast.

The second story says that the first weaver learned his skill by watching a spider as it spun its web. This happened during the reign of their first king, Osei Tutu (1690–1712). Anansi, the spider, is an important figure in Asante folklore, symbolizing trickery and wisdom.

A Danish trader wrote the first account of kente cloth in 1730. He described how silk blankets, imported from Europe, were carefully unraveled. The silk thread was used to produce the best

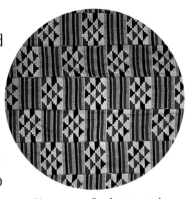

Close up of a kente strip.

kente cloths, which were worn by chiefs. Today new fibers, such as rayon, have replaced silk, though cotton is still used.

Ewé weavers often produce cloths with images, such as cows, horses, and sheep, as well as human figures, trees, flowers, and household objects. As many as 70 different motifs can appear on one cloth. Asante weavers prefer regular balanced patterns. They often use bright colors, especially reds and yellows.

Hammock made by the Ewé people.

45

FIND OUT MORE

AFRICAN CRAFTS

Duncan Clarke. *The Art of African Textiles*. (Grange, 2002).

John Gillow. *Printed and Dyed Textiles from Africa*. (British Museum Press, 2001).

R. Jewell. *African Designs*. (British Museum Press, 1994).

Loeb, Slight & Stanley. *Designs We Live By: An Eyewitness Guide*. (NSEAD, 1993).

John Mack (ed). *Masks: The Art of Expression*. (British Museum Press, 1994).

John Picton & John Mack. *African Textiles*. (British Museum Press, 1989).

Frank Willett. *African Art*. (Thames & Hudson, 1986).

You may have to ask your local library to order these books.

DESIGNS TO COPY

Mira Bartok, Christine Ronan, Esther Grisham. *West Africa: Ghana*. (Stencils) (Collins Educational, 1992).

Gregory Mirow. *Traditional African Designs*. (Dover, 1997).

Geoffrey Williams. *African Designs from Traditional Sources*. (Dover, 1971).

MYTHS AND LEGENDS

Adwoa Badoe. *The Pot of Wisdom: Ananse Stories*. (Groundwood, 2001).

Martin Bennett. *West African Trickster Tales*. (Oxford University Press, 1994).

Alastair Campbell. *Anansi*. (Stanley Thomas. 1999).

Deborah Chocolate. *Talk Talk: An Asante Legend*. (Legends of the World) (Troll, 1993).

Greaves. *When Hippo Was Hairy: And Other Tales from Africa*. (Southern Book Publishers, 1988).

Gerald McDermott. *Anansi the Spider*. (Hamilton, 1973).

Margaret Musgrove. *The Spider Weaver: A Legend of Kente Cloth*. (Scholastic, 2001).

Cynthia Rider. *Anansi Traps a Snake*. (Oxford University Press, 1999).

Joanna Troughton. *Anansi & The Magic Yams*. (Blackie, 1994).

Lyall Watson. *Warriors, Warthogs and Wisdom: Growing up in Africa*. (Kingfisher, 1997).

MEET THE PEOPLE

Alison Brownlie. *A Flavour of West Africa*. (Food and Festivals) (Hodder Wayland, 2002).

J. Peffer Engels. *Benin Kingdom of West Africa*. (Celebrating the Peoples & Civilizations of Africa) (Rosen, 1999).

Philip Koslow. *Centuries of Greatness: The West African Kingdoms 750–1900*. (Chelsea House, 1998).

Carol Thompson. *The Asante Kingdom*. (African Civilizations) (Franklin Watts, 1999).

Francis Provencal, Catherine McNamara. *A Child's Day in a Ghanaian City*. (Benchmark Books, 2001).

Mary Quigley. *Ancient West African Kingdoms: Ghana, Mali, & Songhai*. (Understanding People in the Past) (Heinemann, 2002).

LISTEN TO THESE

Stories from Africa told by Janet Suzman (Audio Cassette, Ivory Shell Audio Tapes, 1999).

Africa: The Very Best of Africa (Music CD, Nascente). The best starting point to find out about the music of Africa.

Ali Farka Toure & Ry Cooder. *Talking Timbuktu* (Music CD, World Circuit). A celebrated musician from Mali meets an American bluesman.

Manu Dibango. *The Very Best of* (Music CD, Manteca). Afro-soul-jazz fusion.

Orchestra Baobab. *Specialist in All Styles* (Music CD, World Circuit). One of the greatest African bands of all time returns with its original lineup and a new landmark album.

SOME WEB SITES TO VISIT

British Museum
www.thebritishmuseum.ac.uk
Features over 5,000 objects showing the enormous range of the British Museum's collections. The families and children section includes games, activities and quizzes, noticeboards displaying work, and an "Ask the Expert" facility.

African Art Museum
www.zyama.com
This collection of African tribal art can show you over 1,200 statues, masks, religious and domestic objects, furniture, and weapons. Discover the art and history of more than 100 African peoples.

Art & Life in Africa
http://www.uiowa.edu/~africart
A huge site, based in Iowa, with lots of interesting features and plenty of useful links to other Web sites dealing with African arts and crafts.

The Story of Africa
http://www.bbc.co.uk/worldservice/africa/features/storyofafrica
Tells the history of the continent from an African perspective, showing the events and characters that have shaped the continent from the origins of humankind to the end of apartheid.

SOME MUSEUMS TO VISIT

National Museum of African Art Smithsonian Institution
950 Independence Avenue, SW
Washington, D.C. 20560
(202) 633-4600

American Museum of Natural History
Central Park West at 79th Street
New York, NY 10024
(212) 769-5100

Fowler Museum of Cultural History, UCLA
W Sunset Blvd & Westwood Plz
Los Angeles, CA 90077
(310) 825-4361

The Field Museum
1400 S. Lake Shore Dr.
Chicago, IL 60605
(312) 922-9410

INDEX